RAPTURE

When Is It?

BY: Arthur Treats

Rapture: When Is It?
Table of Contents

Prelude

Before I get into this fairly short teaching, just let me say this. Through the years there have been theories about when the rapture will occur. Believe it or not, I think I can understand why people might do this. There are two main reasons, maybe more; one of those reasons is to fool mankind.

> "Jesus answered: 'Watch out that no one deceives you. For many will come in my name, claiming, '"I am the Messiah," and will deceive many,'" (Matthew 24:4-5 *New International Version*).

And the other reason is simply that they are Christians and they are desirous to be in heaven.

"He said to them: 'It is not for you to know the times or dates the Father has set by his own authority,'" (Acts 1:7 *New International Version*).

So, whatever the reason these people are deceived when the make their predictions. They are deceived because of a lack of knowledge of what Jesus said. Therefore, having the desire the go to heaven myself, but knowing what Jesus had said, I will give you a little teaching about the rapture.

CHAPTER 1
What Does it Mean?

The word rapture means exceeding great joy; although, I heard that it is a Latin word for the catching away of the saints. When I think about the time when Jesus comes to take His own obedient saints to heaven I think of the most joyous time for the Christians; that time is the rapture. So, whether you choose to believe the rapture to mean the catching away of the saints, as people use it from the Latin, or you think of the rapture as a time of great exceeding joy, which will happen when the Christians are caught up to heaven, we're talking about the same thing.

"For the Lord himself will come down from heaven, with a loud command, with the voice of the archangel and with the trumpet call of God, and the dead in Christ will rise first. After that, we who are still alive and are left will be caught up together with them in the clouds to meet the Lord in the air. And so we will be with the Lord forever," (1 Thessalonians 4:16-17 *New International Version*).

Of coarse, if he was talking about Jesus coming for those in Christ who have died in faith then he must also be talking about those left alive who are in Christ. This will be the most joyous time for the Christian.

When is The Rapture?

There was a book published back in 1988 about why the rapture was going to occur then. There has been much controversy over it because Jesus said that no man will know the day or hour. And that it true that we will not know the day nor hour, but only the season; but he probably took the words that were translated as day or hour too literally; the truth is that no man knows the time.

"He said to them: 'It is not for you to know the times or dates the Father has set by his own authority,'" (Acts 1:7 *New International Version*).

Some versions of Matthew 24:36 say that people won't know the **exact** day and hour, but that would not sound right when compared with Acts 1:7.

"And early in the morning you say, 'It is going to rain, because the sky is red and dark.' You can predict the weather by looking at the sky, but you cannot interpret the signs concerning these times!" (Matthew 16:3 *Good News Translation*).

The person who wrote about the rapture would happen in 1988 might have been thinking about his own mortal life on earth being at its end, he might have been thinking, *'The doctor gave me one year to live, and the will be in 1988, so maybe I'll just say that the rapture will happen then.'*

I remember hearing Paul Crouch from TBN saying that some guy made a prediction that the rapture would be *mm,dd,yyyy*; Paul said he wanted to interview that guy the next day.

R.W. Shamback said that he could tell you the hour that Jesus is coming, he kind of said it humorously. He looked straight into the camera, pointed at the TV audience and said that He will come when you don't think He will. That is so true.

Take a lessen from ancient Israel. They got tired of waiting for the Messiah before He came, or they set their own molds of what He would be like. When He came He didn't fit those molds, and those who were tired of waiting didn't realize that He was there. They thought it was going to be an endless wait; either that, or when He came He wasn't what they thought He should be. But, out of all that, some did see Him for who He really was; those were the unschooled.

So, what Jesus was saying in all this is that knowing the specific day, month, year, (even) decade, is not necessary for you, and probably not even going to happen. But, what we should be able to do is look at the events around us, who's president, what's happening in the weather, what is going on in the media, the world's reaction to the word of God, things like that and know that Jesus is soon to come back for His obedient ones. Again I say, it is not for you or me to know or even worry about specific times that God has set by His awesome authority; what you and I must do—and I do mean must—is that we must be ready.

And what does being ready include? It includes being willing and obedient (Isaiah 1:19), growing in His word and learning, and watching for His coming.

CHAPTER 2
Life of Obedience

Let me start this chapter off with a story. When Jake was born he was born into a very important family. His father, being a head of state, had to travel most of the time so he left instructions for Jakes guardians and teachers. Now, Jake had to learn the life of obedience; the alternative was not something to be desired. Oh, Jake's big brother was working with his father.

Jake could read those instructions for himself, his father provided a copy for him, and if he didn't understand something he could always call his father and ask what he meant. See, Jake's guardians and teachers did not always tell Jake the whole truth, and sometimes they might even blatantly lie. But it was always Jake's aspiration to go where his father was, be like his big brother.

Ok, you might have figured that parable out; if you haven't yet, I'll give you a little time. But while you're thinking about it please read this; it might help you with that parable.

When you were born your father had certain rules of thumb for you and your brothers to do. Suppose your father was a good man, which I hope he was or is, but you decided to go your own way and do your own thing. What would he think of that? Well, of course he would still love you, you're his child. But would he cater to your wishes; if you asked him for a car when you graduated from high school would he honor that request (remember, you are a disobedient boy or girl)?

Then came the time when you left home saying, "Yeah, dad, I am your kid, but I don't like these rules. I'm leaving." Soon your family moved with your father, but no one told you. Well, why should they tell you? He might give you his number and address, but...

If you need more time to think about the parable, stop reading, but then come back to this when you're ready. Ok, when you were born again God became your Father, your heavenly Father. God is a very, very important person (entity), actually, the most important in the universe; and your older brother, Jesus, travels with Him. When you were born into this family you were given a copy of the instructions that He gave to all of His children. He also gave you guardians—pastors—and teachers and others to help you grow. These pastors and teachers *et al* can teach and often do teach half-truths and lies, so you can and should check out what they are telling you. But, even then, some of you try to blend in with the rest of the world, maybe even using the excuse that, "Paul became a Greek to win the Greeks." You just don't want the world to look at you as strange.

> "But ye are a chosen generation, a royal priesthood, an holy nation, a peculiar people; that ye should shew forth the praises of him who hath called you out of darkness into his marvellous light;" (1 Peter 2:9 *King James Version*).

The word **peculiar** means strange. People of the world will call us different, weird, peculiar, strange. It's not our aim to be thought of as weird or strange, but a son or daughter of God (lives in the world, but is not of the world) is strange to those of the world.

How do you show others that you have submitted your life to your heavenly Father, to Jesus and to the Holy Spirit? How do you promote the love of God, which you should be living? How does anyone know that you truly believe Jesus and His word?

> "Verily, verily, I say unto you, He that believeth on me, the works that I do shall he do also; and greater works than these shall he do; because I go unto my Father," (John 14:12 *King James Version*). Read the next verse, this verse is the condition to the promise.

The word **normal** came to me; my dad and I used to joke around with this word a lot back in the early 80's. **Normal** means to be conformed to the way everyone else is doing it (the status-quo). You are blessed if you are doing things God's way and the people of the world call you abnormal (not normal).

When I was in school, before I was born again, I was belittled because I was different in the fact that I was a pacifist and was afraid to fight; almost everyone in my class was a bully where I was concerned. But, just after I was born again I stood up to the biggest, baddest, bully is the school to protect a freshman whom I didn't know, and he backed down; later on I realized that it wasn't me but Jesus in me, because I wouldn't have done that. And that was a one-time event, not to be repeated.

My life didn't seem to change until I was baptized in the Holy Spirit 4 years later. Oh, I read my Bible, but I just didn't get it, and no pastor helped me out. But the Holy Spirit is the teacher.

> "But the Comforter, which is the Holy Ghost **(Holy Spirit)**, whom the Father will send in my name, he shall teach you all things, and bring all things to your remembrance, whatsoever I have said unto you." (John 14:26 *King James Version*).

Jesus was my Lord for 4 years before I received this baptism, but I hadn't changed. I was still doing things like the world, thinking like the world, talking like the world (I was never a cusser); and I was going to "Bible studies". Why did I quote Bible studies? Because, although people might have brought their Bibles, rarely was the topic Holy Spirit centered. The Holy Spirit is the author of the Bible.

You might be reading this and thinking to yourself, *'I made Jesus my Lord in _____, but I have always known that there must be something more to it.'* or *'I just wish I could understand the Bible better. My pastor tells me I'll never understand it, but that's got to be wrong.'* Well, you're right, you can understand the Bible. Just ask God, your heavenly Father, in the name of Jesus, for the baptism in the Holy Spirit. Be specific and use the words. Use these words, "Father, in Jesus' name, please baptize me in the Holy Spirit." You will have the urge to speak out in, what sounds like, gibberish. Don't worry, let it out; that's called unknown tongues and it's fine. But, before you do this you must be committed to Jesu

CHAPTER 3
Growth

At the point a person is born again a new life has begun. If that man walks out of the place where he was born again and gets hit by a car and dies, will he go to heaven? Yes, he will. But, if that man were to live for many more years then he would be required to do some things, they are the things that Jesus did and spoke of, such as what He told His disciples in Mark 16:15-18.

"He gave them these orders, "Go, take this message of my love and peace to all creation. Those people who decide to put their faith in me because of your word and/or what they see and are baptized will join me in heaven one of these days *if they continue in it*, but whoever comes but does not continue in their faith or doesn't come at all will not join me in heaven. Do you understand?

"Those who are honest in their faith in my word will take my name and drive them evil demons out of those who need it. They will also lay their hands on sick folk, it doesn't matter what the sickness because it's not from me or my Father; do this and the sick will recover, whether you see it or not. If there is a reason that you must pick up a snake—not just tempting the Lord because that's sin—and the snake bites you it will not harm you because you belong to me/Us. The same goes for drinking anything deadly, or eating anything deadly, it won't harm you. But, now this is crucial, you must wait for the baptism and the anointing in the Holy Spirit before you can do any of this; and you will also speak in new, unlearned, tongues," (*Steadfast in Honor*).

Now, some versions of the Bible say that Mark 16:15-20 are not in the original manuscript, as if they really had seen the original manuscript which was destroyed probably back in the 4th or 5th century. Even if it were true that this portion of scripture was not in the original manuscript, it is a simple expansion on what Jesus was talking about in John 14:12; and there Jesus even gives a promise also.

"Very truly I tell you, whoever believes in me will do the works I have been doing, and they will do even greater things than these, because I am going to the Father. And I will do whatever you ask in my name, so that the Father may be glorified in the Son," (John 14:12-13 *New International Version*).

The works that Jesus did were healing the sick, casting out demons, speaking/praying in tongues. He may have had incidences were He had to pick up snakes, and since many didn't like Him He may have been poisoned. He was baptized in the Holy Spirit (Acts 10:38); actually, He was baptized in the Holy Spirit before He did any of this. He could preach before He was baptized, I just don't know that He did.

The title of this chapter is Growth; that is because you must grow into this knowledge before you can step out and actually do these things. To know what Jesus did you must read what He did, and you will find that In the Bible. But, once you have found what He did you have the responsibility of implementing it into your own life and doing it when the need is brought to you.

As I said at the beginning of this section, if a man gets born again then gets killed right away he is going to heaven, but if he doesn't get killed for several years he has the responsibility of growing and doing. See, being born means starting your life, now you must grow, learn and do.

Just so, being born again means starting your 'new' life, now you must grow, learn and do. If you shirk your responsibilities, you are shirking your rights.

Live It

Does you dog ever, "Meow?" Has he ever gotten into the driver's seat of you car and driven himself to the grocery store for food? If your answer to either of these question is "Yes" then you've got serious problems with your dog. Dogs don't do that, they can't, they're dogs.

Are you a Christian, a true disciple of Jesus *the* Christ? Christian literally means one who is of Christ or disciple of Jesus. A Christian is not one who does things according to the standards of the world, surprise!

> "Don't copy the behavior and customs of this world, but let God transform you into a new person by changing the way you think. Then you will learn to know God's will for you, which is good and pleasing and perfect," (Romans 12:2 *New Living Translation*).

If all you had to do in order to get 'your ticket' to heaven was to make Jesus your savior, then the New Testament would be one page and would fit in your shirt pocket, without being folded. But, it's not; is it? The acronym given for the Bible—the Christian Bible—is Basic Instructions Before Leaving Earth. Did you get it, Instruction**s**, there is an s there, that means that it isn't just one instruction but many.

> "And when he had found him, he brought him back to Antioch. For a whole year they assembled together with *and* were guests of the church and instructed a large number of people; and in Antioch the disciples were first called Christians," (Acts 11:26 *Amplified Bible*).

Look at those last six words, "the disciples were first called Christians." Now, why do you think they were called Christians? Was it because they said they were disciples of Jesus Christ? No. The Lord just dropped this into my heart; Antioch was a predominantly Jewish town and the Jews, if you will remember, were always after Jesus to give a sign to show that He was whom He was.

> "So Jesus said to those Jews who had believed in Him, If you abide in My word [hold fast to My teachings and live in accordance with them], you are truly My disciples," (John 8:31 *Amplified Bible*).

21

So, these Jews at Antioch had to see these disciples do something to know that they were truly disciples of Jesus—Jesus, who did things. So, if you're a cat, do things the way a cat would (cats are disciples of the cat); if you are a dog do things the way the dog would. But, you are not cats and dogs. If you are of the world you will do things the way the world does them, according to the standards of the world (the world is predominantly run by the devil). But, if you are a disciple of Jesus, who is *the* Christ, then you should be doing things and living according to the way that your master does, or did, them,

Now, I'm not going to judge you, whether you are truly a disciple of Jesus or not (I could have taken that right, just as they did at Antioch), but there is One who will, besides yourself, of course.

So, if you don't want God to judge you of not being who you say you are, a Christian, then find out what Jesus, your Lord and Master, did and do it. A disciple not only takes in the information that he teacher imparts, but he also does what his teacher does. And, if Jesus did it as a man under the Abrahamic covenant, baptized in the Holy Spirit, then so can you as a man under the Jesus covenant, baptized in the Holy Spirit.

CHAPTER 4
Watch And be Ready

Now, as you are growing in Christ and living the life of a disciple, showing that you are a disciple, not being boastful or self-prideful, you should be watching. "Watching for what?" you might ask.

To answer that question let me ask you: What were the Jews looking for when the Messiah appeared? Some were looking for a political deliverer; others were looking for something else. Some had given up and were trying to cope with their life the way it was.

> "Two women will be grinding with a hand mill; one will be taken and the other left. Therefore keep watch, because you do not know on what day your Lord will come," (Matthew 24:41-42 *New International Version*).

The word **watch** intimates something that you will see, saying that if we must watch for His returning then we will have to know what that will look like. For many decades, probably since Jesus had gone up to heaven, people were trying to grasp what He would look like when He comes in the rapture, actually, when He comes to Earth the next time He comes. When He comes for you, you will know what He looks like; you will just know, I can't tell you how but you will know.

In the rapture, as the Apostle Paul said, we will meet Jesus in the air; so, He won't be coming all the way to the Earth. Now, the same principle goes into effect, although it may not be literally watching; you will still have to be ready.

Paul said that there will be the trumpet of God and the voice of the archangel; I thinking that these things are spiritual. Therefore, you will not be able to hear them in the natural. Only His sheep will be able to discern them and hear His voice.

> "When he has brought out all his own, he goes on ahead of them, and his sheep follow him because they know his voice," (John 10:4 *New International Version*).

I am not going to tell you what you have to do to become His sheep, His true disciples, God's true sons and daughters, but I will say that there is no way to do that until you start with Jesus as Lord. Many churches were preaching that you couldn't do enough good works to get God's favor and a ticket to heaven; you need Jesus. Jesus, Himself, said that the works that God requires is that you believe in Jesus. But, then you need to find out what God calls believing in Jesus. Look at John 14:12 were Jesus equated believing with doing. Then look at Romans 4:17 where Paul equated believing with copying; Abraham believed God, so he called himself what God called him, before there was evidence.

Jesus obeyed God and was baptized in water and the Holy Spirit, then He began doing what God called Him to do. Now look at your life, what are you doing about Jesus, being baptized in water, being baptized in the Holy Spirit, or doing what He has called you to do? Remember, what He has called you to do includes what is written.

www.ingramcontent.com/pod-product-compliance
Lightning Source LLC
Chambersburg PA
CBHW030013040426
42337CB00012BA/763